The Gospel According to Aunt Mildred

Stories of Faith and Family

By Delmer Chilton

with John Fairless

©2016

Lectionary Lab Press

Stories: Windows on Our Lives

[from John]

One of the most iconic lines from the Paul Newman movie, *Cool Hand Luke*, comes from the mouth of The Captain, a prison warden trying to explain the subtleties of prison life on an Alabama chain gang to Newman's stubborn character, who will not stop seeking to escape– "What we've got here is a failure to *communicate*!"

Finding ways to *communicate* is what both of us – Delmer and John – do for a living. For us, it's actually a calling. And we both know something that great communicators from time immemorial have known: if you want people to listen and understand, tell them a story.

Delmer Chilton is one of the most gifted storytellers that I have ever had the privilege to know. Working with him over the past 20 years or so, I have come to know the stories of his family and various life situations that he has encountered almost as well as he does. When we are together with a group, I often say, "Tell them the one about...."

I have laughed and cried -- and laughed till I cried – at many of the stories in this book. While most of the stories were originally told in the context of sermons, they are offered here simply as they are, with very little comment and no Bible verses at all. If you would like to attach a meaning, spiritual or otherwise, to them – please do.

Or, you can just enjoy them or ponder them or scratch your head at them – "whatever floats your boat," as a character from my past used to say. We thank you for listening and sharing the story with us.

As Octavia Butler, an award-winning science fiction author, once said: "Every story I create, creates me."

Well, there you go.

[from Delmer]

People sometimes ask who taught me to tell stories. I tell them "If anybody did, it was my grandfather Reid Chilton." But he didn't do it on purpose, it just kind of happened. He had a wry sense of humor, and eyes and ears that paid attention to telling details. He told stories as he moved through his day and I tagged along listening. To me, all good stories started with "I recollect . . .," not "Once upon a time …. "

I also learned while sitting on the front porch of a Sunday afternoon, or around the kitchen table late into Saturday night, listening as my parents chatted with visiting friends and relatives. A variety of religious, social, and political opinions were put forth using stories rooted in family history and local legend.

After several haphazard attempts to teach others to tell stories, I have concluded that storytelling is not so much taught as *learnt*. One learns by listening to others tell their stories, either out loud or on paper. Storytelling is ninety percent listening – it's really only about ten percent telling.

Back in the early 1990s, my congregation printed out copies of my sermons to send to shut-ins. Graciously, they put my parents, back on the farm in North Carolina, on the mailing list. My Mama and Daddy read them when they came, and then Mama added them to the stack on a shelf in a kitchen cabinet.

One summer my sister came from her home in Oregon to visit for a few weeks. One afternoon she took down the stack and read most of the sermons. She told my mother, "I remember all those things happening. I just didn't know they meant anything."

Well they didn't mean anything, to her. They meant something to me – that's the nature of memory and story.

Speaking of memory, many of the people in these stories are still alive and may not remember these things the way I do. That's okay. I've been married to Deborah for over forty years. Someone told us recently, "Isn't that great, you have forty years of shared memories."

After talking it over a bit, we decided we have over forty years of shared experiences – which we remember differently.

Part 1: Growing Up

We're not sure if it's just a "Southern thing" or not, but down here, when we meet a person for the first time, one of the things we are eager to know is where you're from – which isn't necessarily the same thing as where you are currently living.

Rather, we want to know who your people are, what the formative cultural influences on your life were, what kind of things we might want to watch out for if we are going to be spending any significant amount of time with you -- in other words, we want to know where you grew up.

You see, *where* you grew up says a lot about *how* you grew up; and, more than likely, it gives us some clues about just how much we're going to like you and trust you – or maybe not.

Either way, it's important.

And you can trust us on that.

YOU MIGHT NEED IT

My daddy's sister, Aunt Mildred, never, ever really threw anything away. When her nieces and nephews complained to her about this, she would say, "You just never know when you might need it."

Our protests that you had to be able to find "it" in order to use "it" when you needed "it," fell on deaf ears. She was confident that she knew where all her "its" were.

And I think she did.

I would ask her about a bill or a letter or a magazine and she would say something like, "It's in the back bedroom, in the left-hand corner of the closet, third shoebox from the bottom, in a plastic bag."

And she'd be right.

God is, I think, a bit like Aunt Mildred; if not southern then at least eccentric.

STUMPED

There's a favorite story in my family about my grandfather Reid Chilton, who was just absolutely crazy about playing baseball.

When he was a teen-ager, he lived with and worked for his uncle, a holiness preacher who didn't hold with the foolishness of ball playing. One day, Uncle Arrington knew that Reid was scheduled to play in a baseball game, so he put him to working sowing peas in the cornfield. (For the non-gardeners: this was a common practice years ago, pea vines didn't harm the corn and grew up wrapped around the stalk.) Uncle Arrington said, "Finish sowing those peas and you can go."

Reid was devastated, he knew he didn't have time to plant that whole bucket of peas and ride his mule over to Dry Pond for the ball game. As he worked and fretted, he came upon a burned out stump in the middle of the field. He looked around, saw no one was looking, dumped that whole bucket of peas in the stump and covered them with dirt. He ran out of the field, showed the good reverend his empty bucket and rode off to play ball.

Things were fine until several weeks later when Uncle Arrington was cultivating the field and came upon a stump over-flowing with pea vines!

Grandpa always finished that story by looking wistfully into the distance and muttering, "Who knew peas would grow in a stump?"

MRS. GAMMONS

Her name was Mrs. Gammons. I don't remember her first name, but I do remember her: she was my Sunday School teacher.

Mrs. Gammons was a shy, quiet, reserved woman. With her graying hair done up in a stiff, 60's up-do and wearing a simple gray or blue dress, she looked a lot like Aunt Bea from *The Andy Griffith Show*.

Mrs. Gammons suffered patiently the indignities heaped upon her by a rather uninterested and unruly gang of farm boys. We hid stray cats and dogs under her desk and threw tiny spit-balls into her hair when she had her back turned to write on the board.

And, miracle of miracles, week after week, she came back to try again.

She had no particular talent for the job; she had never read a book on Christian Education, nor had she ever been to a teacher's workshop. She just came in each week and took the roll, putting a Gold Star beside our name for attendance, Bible brought, offering given, and memory verse learned.

After the paperwork was completed, the lesson began. First we read the scripture, then paragraph by paragraph we would take turns reading the lesson out loud. Mrs. Gammons would help us with the hard words and at the end of each paragraph she would sum up the meaning and ask us if we had any questions.

We never did.

This went on for 45 minutes or so, and then we were done — mercifully for us and, I imagine, for her.

But sometimes we finished early, before the bell, and she would just stare at us with the look of someone who wished to be someplace, any place, else.

She would look up at the ceiling, as if by wishing she could make the bell ring, then she would look at us, and sigh, and THEN:

She would sigh again, and begin haltingly, in her gentle soft voice, to tell us about Jesus. She told us about how much he meant in her life, about what a loving, kind, gentle and comforting presence He had been for her in times of hurt and sorrow.

She talked about how Jesus challenges us, dares us, leads us and helps us to be better people; better in how we treat others, and better in how we treat ourselves.

This was during the 60's and while many others in our community were saying extremely hateful and racist things, she told us that Jesus loved black people as much as he loved us, and that we ought to love black people, too, and treat them right.

She said that Jesus lived forgiveness and taught forgiveness and that since Jesus had forgiven our mistakes and sins, that we ought to forgive the mistakes and sins of others.

And somehow, not really knowing how or when it happened, when my time in Mrs. Gammons' class was over, I discovered that I was in love with Jesus, a love that has never left me in the 40-plus years since.

In seminary I learned a lot of things I never learned in Sunday School, but I never had to unlearn anything I learned from Mrs. Gammons.

It's all true.

COWBOY BOB

When I was 5-10 years old, my favorite TV show was "The Cowboy Bob Show" (or something like that, it was about 50 years ago). It was a local show, on Saturday after the early morning cartoons. Cowboy Bob wore a stereotypical Western shirt and white Stetson and sat behind a table where he demonstrated card tricks and simple science projects in between episodes of old 1930s, serial westerns starring people like Lash LaRue and Hop-along Cassidy. Cowboy Bob was my hero.

One day at school, I heard great news. "Glad tiding of exceeding great joy," at least for a third-grade boy with a cowboy fixation; Cowboy Bob was coming to town! He was going to be in the annual Mount Airy Christmas parade on the Friday after Thanksgiving. I was agog with excitement, I made a calendar and marked off the days, just like I had seen one of my heroes do in a western, (except I used a red crayon and I'm pretty sure he used his own blood).

Finally, the day arrived. I persuaded my 6'3" father to let me sit on his shoulders so I could get a really good look when Cowboy Bob rolled through on his float. After too many clowns and Cub Scout troops and church floats and high school bands for my taste, here he was, on the back of a flatbed truck – the floor covered with scattered hay, a few bales with little kids sitting on them and a short, paunchy man lamely spinning a rope and waving at the crowd. The wind almost blew his hat off and for a moment I could see that he was bald. I have never been so disappointed in my life. "Who is that?" I cried to my father, "That can't be Cowboy Bob!"

But alas, it was; it really was.

DADDY, DADDY, DADDY

When I was about 12 or 13 I was in the Boy Scouts. One night at Scouts we were running a race and I tripped. I fell face down in gravel on the side of the road. I lodged a piece of gravel under the skin on my forehead.

The rural medical clinic was a mile or so down the road from our meeting place. The Doctor and my father were both assistant Scoutmasters so they gathered me up and took me to the clinic.

The doctor was good but his bedside manner was a bit on the brusque side. As I lay there on that cold, hard metal table he came at me with a huge needle to numb my forehead. I am still not very fond of needles, but then I was deathly afraid of them.

I looked over at my Daddy and began to cry out, "Daddy, Daddy, daddy, please Daddy. Don't let him hurt me, please Daddy. Daddy, Daddy, Daddy."

The doctor threw a leg over me to hold me down, put his left arm down on my chest and proceeded to inject the needle. All the while I continued to cry and beg and plead for my Daddy to make him stop. And just as the needle entered I saw my Daddy's hands, knuckles white as he clutched my jacket. I looked up and saw a tear in the corner of his eye. It was the only time I ever, ever saw him cry.

Daddy, Daddy, Daddy.

THE VOICE OF GOD

I grew up next door to my Grandparents and ate breakfast with them 3 or 4 times a week, which was good, because Aunt Mildred lived with them and was a great cook and made especially wonderful biscuits; but it was bad because you could not talk during breakfast because the folks, Grandpa and Grandma and Aunt Mildred, had to listen to their favorite program while they ate:

THE MOODYS OBITUARY COLUMN OF THE AIR!

It started with somber, funereal organ music, then a deep, *basso profundo* voice would intone,

> *John Doe of 334 Mockingbird Lane passed away last evening at Northern Surry Hospital. He is survived by . . .He was employed by . . .. He was a member of . . .. Funeral to be held at . . . conducted by the Rev. . . .Memorials may be sent to . . .. etc.*

for about 5 to 10 names, all read with great dignity by that deep, deep voice.

I was about 5 or 6 at the time and concluded that the voice on the radio was the voice of God.

Who else would know all those things about a person, all those details?

And the Church we attended then put a lot of stress on the Second Coming and the Rapture and the *"He Will come Like A Thief In the Night"* and stuff like that.

They really talked a lot about whether or not you'd be ready to go when the Man Upstairs decided it was your turn to face the Final Judgment.

So, I decided the voice on the radio was God sending out a message: "These are the ones I took last night. Are you ready to meet your maker?"

One day, my Daddy dropped me off at Elmer's Barber Shop to get a haircut while he ran over to town to get a truckload of fertilizer.

I had just learned to read a bit and was very happily looking through the Boys Life magazines when I got scared out of my skin.

The man in the chair opened his mouth and out came that oh so familiar voice:

"Elmer, could you take a little more off around the ears?"

Oh my God, Yes MY GOD was there, right there with me in that Barber Shop.

Oh no! My time had come! He had come to take me home. It was time for me to face the Final Judgment.

And of one thing I was never more certain; I was not ready to go.

So, I hid in the bathroom until he left, cowering in the dark under the sink.

THE BASEMENT

The old farm house where I grew up had an old dirt basement underneath the kitchen, more like what people in other parts of the country refer to as a root cellar. You had to go outside to get to it, going through an entrance that always reminded me of the storm shelter in THE WIZARD OF OZ.

For much of the year we used it to store potatoes and yams and apples. They were in old wooden crates on a low table against the back wall, covered with burlap sacks.

Two or three times a week, Mama would send me to the basement to get something for her. I knew that old basement so well that I never turned on the light; I just walked straight into the darkness to the appropriate box and scooped up whatever it was that Mama wanted.

One year I got a flashlight for Christmas. For a few days I did nothing but fiddle with that flashlight. I did Morse Code with Cousin Bob next door, I tried to scare my little sister with the flashlight in the mouth trick, I tired reflecting light off household mirrors into people's eyes to annoy them; the usual 9-year-old boy stuff.

Well, when my mother sent me to the basement for potatoes I of course took my flashlight. I stepped into the basement and turned it on . . . and immediately wished I hadn't.

In the sudden glare of my flashlight, I saw several rats and bugs and a snake or two scurry back into their hiding places.

I shuddered to think of all the times I had been down there in the dark and all those icky things were all around me and because it was dark I didn't see them.

In this case the shining of the light was not very comforting to me, instead it scared me greatly.

WRESTLING AND THE RESURRECTION

When I was in elementary school one of my favorite programs was what my brother and I called "The Wrestling Show." Whenever it was on, we parked ourselves on the floor as close as possible to the television set to cheer on our heroes Johnny Weaver and George Becker as they battled the evil Rip Hawk and Swede Hansen.

This was real low-rent entertainment, nothing like the arena spectacles they show now. There was just a wrestling ring in a room in the High Point NC TV studio, with a couple of rows of fans sitting in folding chairs on one side. The announcer was Charlie Harville, who also did the local sports news and play-by-play at high school football games and the occasional supermarket ad.

When I got older I figured out that the matches were carefully scripted morality plays in which you could rely on the bad guys to be gleefully nasty and to always cheat and the good guys to be clean-cut and moral and admirable representatives of truth, justice and the American way; but when I was nine it was all very, very real and very, very exciting.

The script always went like this.

Things would start out even, then the good guys would start to get the upper hand, then the bad guys would start cheating, the good guys were being thrown around the ring like rag dolls, one of the bad guys would put the good guy's head between the ropes, the other bad guy would get out of the ring and grab a chair and hit the good guy with it.

All the while the announcer would be saying things like, "Oh, my goodness!" "This is bad!" "I don't see how Johnny will get out of this." Then one of the bad guys would pin the good guy on the floor and the referee would start counting the three count and the announcers would say, "He's down, he's out, this is over! There's no way out of this! No! Wait! He's up!" And the good guys would miraculously recover and win.

It may seem silly, but "No! Wait! He's up!" is the first thing I think of every Easter morning. Long after I (mostly) forgot about TV wrestling, I remembered Charlie Harville screaming into the microphone "No! Wait! He's up!" and the startling and exuberant "terror and amazement" of feeling utter and complete sadness and despair transformed into unexpected joy and hope.

JESUS WEPT

When I was a kid going to Sunday School in the Baptist Church you answered the roll with a "memory verse." The line rendered in some modern Bibles as "Jesus began to weep," was only two words in the King James Version: "Jesus wept."

 It was, therefore, a popular memory verse in the Junior Boys Department until the teacher banned it from further usage. For a very long time that verse meant very little to me except as a pleasant memory of boyhood cutesiness.

But not so as I move into my sixties. More and more people that I have known and loved most of my life have died in recent years.

And like Jesus, I have wept. Unlike Jesus, I did not have the power to bring my loved ones back to life.

LIGHTNING AND THE LORD

I had my first real theology lesson when I was about twelve or thirteen I was working in the tobacco field with my father; he was plowing, I was hoeing. It was an unusual day in that we were out there by ourselves; usually there were several of my brothers and sisters and Mama and maybe Aunt Mildred. But not today. Today, it was just us.

I had my head down, concentrating on not hitting a young tobacco plant with my hoe when I realized the tractor was no longer running and Daddy was yelling for me to run to him. He pointed into the distance and then beckoned me with a wave. I looked out across the valley and saw sharp lightning and a wall of rain and hail coming our way. Then I heard the thunder and felt the wind and saw it stir the trees in the woods around the edges of the field. I ran to Daddy and together we ran to the nearest tobacco barn.

We were probably safe, but I didn't feel safe. I felt exposed, sitting just inside the door of a fifty-year-old log barn with a tin roof and a dirt floor. The wind howled and the hail pounded the roof and the thunder roared and the lightning lit up the sky. Daddy sat on an old box, his long legs crossed and wrapped around each other as he took an unfiltered cigarette out of the pack and fumbled for a dry match.

I shivered, from fear or wet or maybe a bit of both and asked him, "Aren't you afraid?" (Full disclosure – I probably said, "Ain't you scared?") And he blew a stream of smoke and looked me in the eye and said, "Yes, I am. But I'm not in charge, he is."(Pointing up with his index finger.) "Comes a point in life, son, where you just have to decide if you trust God or not. I trust him, so I'll sit here 'til this is over and then deal with what's next."

"But, but," I said, "Sometimes it doesn't work out for the best. People get hurt or die." and Daddy said, "I didn't say I understood the Lord, son, I just said I trusted him."

MAMA SPIRIT

A lot of people think the Holy Spirit is sweet and nice and soothing, but I think the Spirit is a lot like my Mama.

When I was a young teenager, Mama and Daddy went to work in the Cotton Mill to supplement the family income. Up until then we got by on just the tobacco crop. They still raised tobacco, they did it after work and on weekends, and expected a lot of help from their children.

They would leave for the mill around 6:30 AM. They would put a list of things to get done in the middle of the table for the children to see when we got up, some to be done around the house, most in the fields. They got home around 3:30. We tried to figure out how long it would take to get the jobs on the list done, then we always waited until the last possible minute to start working.

One day, we had done nothing on the list. It was about 11:00 or 11:30 AM. We were drinking Kool-Aid and eating peanut butter and cracker sandwiches and watching the Dialing for Dollars movie on Channel 8 out of High Point, NC when

> *". . .suddenly, from the kitchen door there came a sound like the rush of a violent wind and it filled the entire room where we were sitting . . . "*

and the name of that wind was Mama and she was some kind of mad.

She had gotten sick at work and came home early, and instead of finding her children busy about the business she had left them to do, she found them sitting around, doing nothing.

Mama roared into the den, the fly swatter she had grabbed off the hook by the kitchen stove in hand. She drove us out of that house, across the yard and up the hill, into the fields where we were supposed to be hoeing tobacco.

We danced into that field – Mama's hand on the back of our neck, swatting at our legs and behinds, while we stretched our feet and bottom as far away from her as we could get to avoid the switch.

Yes, brothers and sisters, I believe the Spirit in Acts, Chapter 2 is a whole lot more like my Mama on a bad day than any sweet, sweet spirit, any gentle breath of God, we might conjure up.

LEFT BEHIND

When I was a child, we had week-long revivals at Slate Mountain Missionary Baptist Church. The revival preacher generally centered on issues of Jesus coming again in judgment. While he spent a lot of time on the lake of fire, most of his effort was put into the rapture and how the Christians would be taken up to heaven and the evil people left behind.

When I was 9 or 10, I was mighty shy and mighty scared of going to hell. If there was any way to get saved and accept Christ and avoid Hellfire other than going down to the front of the church during the invitation, I would have done it. But there wasn't and I was too shy to go down there in front of all those people. So I prayed each night in my bed for forgiveness and please, please Jesus, don't leave me behind.

One morning during the fall revival I awoke at dawn to a completely empty house. My parents and my four siblings weren't there. Even the dog was nowhere to be seen. The electricity wouldn't work. I immediately jumped to conclusions. Oh my God! Jesus came back, and took everybody else, and left me behind. I'm going to hell.

It sounds funny now, but I assure you – it wasn't funny then. Imagine a nine-year-old boy, in his underwear, down on his knees in the frost covered backyard, tears streaming down his face, pleading with Jesus to spare him. It was an awful few minutes.

Then I heard a familiar sound, "Putt, putt, putt." Our farm tractor. Suddenly the dog burst over the hill behind the house followed by the tractor pulling a trailer load of cured tobacco, my family riding along. They had gone to get a load of cured tobacco out of the barn and transfer it to the pack house, and decided that since I had the sniffles to leave me in bed. And, the power had gone out, which happened once or twice a month, for no known reason. Instead of the Devil coming to devour me, it was just my parents coming to fuss at me for being outside in my underwear and my siblings to laugh at me for being afraid.

THE CHICKEN AND THE SNAKE

My grandmother used to get eggs from a family who lived about a mile further down the dirt road by her house. When I was little, five or six, Grandma and I would often walk there to visit on a cool summer's evening.

Eventually we would go out past the hen-house to the spring-house, where they kept the eggs in little wire cages submerged in a concrete tank of water fed by a cold mountain spring.

We put the eggs in little tin buckets padded with dishcloths and walked home for supper; probably bacon and eggs with biscuits, because Grandma wasn't particular about exactly when she had breakfast.

One summer evening, just as we came out of the spring-house, there was an awful fuss in the chicken yard.

A sudden raising of dust, flurry of feathers and scattering of hens and chickens, much screeching and squawking; and then, just as suddenly, things calmed down and an old gray hen emerged from the bushes with a large black snake in her mouth.

It occurred to me that Grandma wasn't the only tough old bird in this neighborhood.

RUDOLPH

One of my mother's favorite stories is about the year I was supposed to sing at the Slate Mountain Baptist Church Christmas program. My mother was the director and some of us were too young to be in the play and she wanted every child to do something so she had all the little kids pick a Christmas song to sing as a sort of prelude to the rest of the program.

I picked "Rudolph the Red-nosed Reindeer" and, over many objections, practiced it day and night around the house. I also faithfully went to church for play practice and sang it to the empty pews. The night of the play came and I walked out to sing and I looked at a hundred or so faces staring back at me and I sang "Rudolph the red-nosed . . ." and then I stopped.

I started again, "Rudolph, the red-nosed . . . "and then I quit again. Finally, I ran off the stage screaming "Mama!" and fell into my mother's arms. I was four and I have seldom sung in public since.

TRUE STORY

When I was a little kid, we lived in a four-room house: Living room, Kitchen, Parent's Bedroom, Children's bedroom, outhouse in the woods. On Christmas Eve, we went to Grandma and Grandpa's for dinner then we came home and went to bed by 9 o'clock, the four of us in one room, all of us under ten.

Daddy always reminded us that if we heard noise in the night we should stay in bed, because Santa would take our presents back if he caught us peeking.

Early on Christmas morning, long before dawn, we slipped from our bedroom to the living room next door. We opened our presents and squealed with delight, our mouths full of candy we found in our stockings. Suddenly we were aware of a presence in the room then we heard a loud noise, like a cow stuck in a barbed wire fence.

We turned and saw upon the couch a large man with white hair and a beard, tall black boots sitting on the floor; he was asleep snoring loudly, his huge belly going up and down in fretful rhythm.

We were, to use a Biblical phrase, "sore afraid," for we were sure we knew who this visitor was. We did the only thing we could do; we gathered up all the toys and candy and hid them in our beds, then we retired there too, cowering in the dark and cold, waiting for him to leave.

A couple of hours later our parents came to see why we were not around the tree. "Is he gone?" we asked. "Is who gone?" they said.

"You know, HIM. Santa," we said.

I thought my mother would die laughing, I really did.

Our visitor was one of Mama's uncles, her mother's brother, a man once described by his own sister as "the most worthless human being God ever devised."

He had showed up around midnight, on foot and a bit tipsy, on Christmas Eve with nowhere to go. And my parents put him to bed in the only place they had, the living room couch in front of the Christmas Tree.

I have seen many Christmas plays and movies, I have heard and preached many Christmas Eve sermons. But none of them has taught me more than what happened the night my parents made sure there was room for one in need, even if he didn't deserve it.

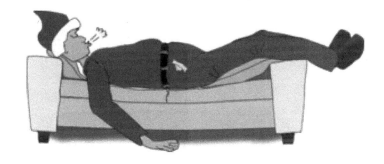

Part 2: Moving Out

Ella Fitzgerald famously sang, "Into each life some rain must fall....*"

She was putting to music the sentiment by the great Henry Wadsworth Longfellow that "the hopes of youth [will] fall thick in the blast;" in other words, there comes a time we all have to move out and move on in life.

Birds from the nest, foxes from their dens, even baby beluga whales in the wide waters of the ocean all leave their mommas and daddies one day. So it is with we humans, too; there comes a time when we set out to make our marks on the world.

With nobody around to keep us from marking the place up, we soon realize the truth that life does have its ups and downs, and that both Wordsworth and Ella were right: some days will be dark and dreary, but on other days the sun will shine.

* written by Allan Roberts (lyrics) and Doris Fisher (melody)

GOING AWAY

I remember the first time I "went away." It was 1972 and I was going away to college. My family is pretty low-key about things like this and there was no special dinner or anything like that. If I remember correctly, I milked the cow as usual that morning, worked in the field with Daddy until noon, then we went to the house for dinner.

(On a southern farm, at noon, it was always "dinner." Lunch was something you ate in the cafeteria at school. And supper is after dark.)

I took a shower, loaded my box of books and my laundry basket full of clothes in the back seat of the car and drove the hour and a half down to Guilford College.

But, I did receive a few "going away" presents. Daddy handed me $10, the first time I remember him giving me money that I had not earned working. Mama gave me a couple of shirts she got on sale. And my cousin Julia (an English teacher) and her husband Sam (a librarian) gave me a Webster's Seventh New Collegiate Dictionary.

I spent the money on gas and wore out the shirts but I still have the dictionary sitting on my bookshelves.

The best going away presents serve two purposes. They are a link to the past and they propel us into the future.

Every time I look up a word in that old dictionary, I remember Julia and Sam's encouragement of my goal of getting a college education; and that dictionary, in its own small way, helped me to achieve that goal.

BACK TO NORMAL

When my son David -- who has now passed both the age of 30 and a height of 6 feet, 9 inches -- was a little-bitty fella, he loved Richard Scarry's *Christmas Book*.

It is a book with no words, just pictures. It shows a traditional New England or Midwestern town going through the Advent season: pictures of families decorating the house, baking and eating cookies and pies.

It shows the town workers putting up lights and decorations downtown and Sunday School folk at Christmas play practice and Santa Claus in the Toy section of the Department Store.

There is a scene of Candlelight Communion and a Christmas Day multigenerational family dinner and then the opening of gifts around the tree and the blazing fireplace.

Throughout the month of December, David — and later my second son, Joseph — would sit on my lap and we would page through this book. The first few times, I told the story; after that the boys took over, narrating and describing the activities on each page.

And, as is the way with all children, each night they said exactly the same thing, in exactly the same way.

The last page was a two-page panorama showing Christmas trees out by the mail-box to be picked up by the garbage man, people going to work, city workers taking down lights and decorations, etc.

At this point, the boys loved to slam the book shut and shout at the top of their lungs: BACK TO NORMAL!

THE TELLING

When my family moved to Nashville, Tennessee, we lived in a three-room apartment on a hill above a strip mall with a grocery store.

Friday night was family night and we went to the grocery to pick out items for home made pizza and desert. This was pre-Blockbuster and the grocery store had a video section where the boys and I picked out the evening's entertainment.

One night I noticed the World War I epic *All Quiet on the Western Front,* shelved among the WESTERNS. I helpfully took it off the shelf and carried it up to the bored teen-ager at the counter and said, "It's an understandable mistake, but this movie isn't a western. It's about World War I and should be shelved among the dramas."

And the kid took it from me and said, "Thank you very much," and placed it under the counter.

The next Friday night, and the next, and the next, this little scenario played itself out. I continued to do it for the somewhat perverse pleasure of it and as an experiment to see if anything ever would change.

After 15 months we bought a house and moved away and changed grocery stores and *All Quiet on the Western Front* was still safely nestled between John Wayne and Clint Eastwood.

But I still had hope.

THE NEW SUIT

I want to tell you a story about my Daddy. His name was Lowell Chilton, born in 1923 on a tobacco farm in Surry County, North Carolina, where he grew up in a little farm house during the Great Depression.

I actually grew up on the same farm, same little house, really. Except that, when Lowell grew up there, the house wasn't finished and was heated by two fireplaces – and the light at night was an oil lantern – and the water was carried into the house in buckets from the spring. And we won't even talk about going to the bathroom.

The family consisted of Lowell and his parents, and his sister, Mildred. They didn't have much and they worked hard for that.

Most of Lowell's clothes were hand-me-downs from relatives; coats and pants and shirts which were ill-fitting and which had worn through or torn, and then had been patched or sewn up. Most boys wouldn't have minded, but Lowell did. He longed to dress nice, to wear something new and stylish, something that fit well and looked good.

One day in the fall, when Lowell was about 8 or 9 years old, his father went to Winston-Salem to sell the tobacco crop. He was gone for several days, because they went the 80-mile round trip in a wagon pulled by mules. Little Lowell sat on the porch waiting for his father to return, and when he saw the wagon coming up the road, he leapt down and rushed out to meet his father.

Running alongside the wagon, he yelled up, "Papa, did you get me anything?" His father smiled, threw down a bag with some fruit and some candy, and then said, "Yep, sure did. I got you a suit of clothes for Christmas from your Mama and me."

Lowell was excited, beside himself with pleasure. "A suit of clothes. Wow!"

He imagined himself with a pair of wing-tip shoes and a four-in-hand tie, just like the people he saw in the pictures in the magazines. "My," he thought, "I will be the best-dressed boy at Slate Mountain Church on Christmas Day, that's for sure!"

He was so excited he could hardly sleep on Christmas Eve. He got up at the break of dawn on Christmas Day, ignoring the slingshot and the yo-yo Santa had brought him; he immediately ripped open the package from his parents. As he looked at the bib overalls and denim jacket that spilled out into his lap, he began to weep.

He got up and went back to bed while his father stared at him – dumbfounded. Papa had meant no harm with his little silly play on words. But, little Lowell was crushed.

Years later, when grown-up Lowell – my Daddy – told me that story, he said, "I know Papa was just playing around, but I had so built up the idea of having a fancy dress suit to wear that nothing else was good enough. It was when he said, 'I got you a suit of clothes' – you know, I would have been very happy with the overalls and the denim jacket."

"Didn't you hear me?"

That's what my Daddy would say when we failed to obey him quickly enough.

"Didn't you hear me?"

That's what my Mama would say when she got home from work and found our chores undone.

"Didn't you hear me?"

That's what the elementary school principal would say when we failed to immediately do whatever it was he told us to do.

I grew up in a world in which it was assumed that children would do what their parents and teachers told them, without grumbling, hesitation or backtalk. Since they could not imagine a child NOT doing as he or she was told, the only excuse they could think of for such failure was not hearing the command, thus, "Didn't you hear me?"

I heard those words a whole lot more than I care to admit or remember. I was not a terribly obedient child, but I was not outwardly rebellious either. I was a bit of a passive-aggressive slacker. So when a parent or teacher or coach or youth minister said, "Didn't you hear me?" I usually responded with something really clever like, "Oh, you meant me?" or "Oh, you meant take out THAT trash can."

No one was ever fooled by this, of course.

One of the distressing things about growing up is that we do indeed become our parents. This has led me to a peculiar and I think unique theory of genetics: I believe that we inherit traits from our parents through our children. I know I didn't become my father until I had two sons.

But, I was not an exact carbon-copy of my father. While, like him, I equated my giving orders to their immediate obedience (oh, silly me); I developed a more modern, ironic, sarcastic approach, as in "exactly what part of 'unload the dishwasher' did you not understand?" But, I think the point is still the same.

QUESTION

Almost 40 years ago I stood in the hallway outside a College Admissions office, sweating uncomfortably in my Sunday Suit and twisting the postcard with the time and place of my appointment in my hands.

I pushed the door open slowly and looked around. I saw a man sitting at his desk, seemingly absorbed in his paperwork. I eased into the room, looking for a place to sit when suddenly he looked up and barked at me, "What are you doing here?"

Startled, I stammered out that I was looking for the Admissions office. He said, "This is it. What are you doing here?"

Again, I attempted to answer. "I'm Delmer Chilton and I have an appointment."

He grunted and said, "I know that, but what are you doing here?"

Know that expression, "Like a deer in the headlights?" That was me. I was completely *bumfuzzled*.

(My grandma used to say that. I really like that word; *bumfuzzled.)*

Finally, I shrugged my shoulders threw up my hands and said, "I don't understand the question. You've got to help me out here!"

Again, the man grunted and said, "What are you doing here? Not here in this room but here in this life? Why do you want to go to college? What is your calling, your purpose, your passion? What are you doing here?"

I don't know how good that man was at recruiting students; but he sure was good at asking important questions.

• •

ELEVATOR

When I was in college, I worked on a tobacco farm in Eastern North Carolina. It was in the early days of mechanized tobacco harvesting and we worked on a contraption, called by some an "elevator," pulled by a tractor through the field.

The harvesters -- "the croppers" we were called -- sat on low seats a few inches from the ground. We "picked" the leaves of the plants and put them in a conveyer belt system that carried them to a platform about 10 feet in the air where the "stringers" tied the leaves onto the tobacco sticks to be hung in the barn for curing.

Our harvester was malfunctioning. The conveyer system wasn't working properly and leaves were dropping out behind us. We kept stopping and starting while trying to fix the machine.

There was a precocious 6-year-old boy who was a friend of the family and was watching us work. He observed our troubles for a while and then walked up to the Farmer and said, "Well, you can't elevate' em all, can you Mr. Virgil?"

WHY

My least favorite part of family road trips was when the boys got into the "Why?" question game. It is the most irritating game on earth. You're not familiar with it? It's really simple and really funny. Well, it's really funny if you're a seven or eight-year-old boy.

All you do is ask your unsuspecting and distracted parent a simple question. Then no matter what the parent says, you respond with "Why?" "When are we stopping for lunch?" "In about an hour." "Why?" "Because we'll be in Morganton and can go to MacDonald's" "Why?" "Because everybody can get something they like at McDonalds" "Why?"

And so on.

The game for the kids is to see how long it takes the parent to figure out what's going on. The game for the parent is see how long they can maintain their carefully arrived-at philosophical position opposing corporal punishment.

As much as it used to irritate me on long road trips, I think "Why?" is the most important question we can ask ourselves.

Didn't someone once say that the "unexamined life is not worth living?"

SPORTS DAD

I learned my most important lesson as a "sports Dad" when my younger son was playing coach-pitch baseball. They weren't a very good team, losing a lot more often than they won.

They were seven years old, and most of them had the attention span of a gnat. They spent more time jostling and picking on each other than paying attention to what was happening on the field.

After the game was over, as they lined up to shake hands with the other team, I would hear the boys ask the coach, "Did we win? Did we win?"

If the coach said "yes," they would cheer, if the coach said "no," they would kick the ground.

And after that they would ask, "What's for snack?"

READY

In the fall of 1976, I began studying for the ministry at Southeastern Baptist Theological Seminary in Wake Forest, NC.

We had chapel every day at about 10 am. Most days a professor or an upper-class student preached; occasionally we had special guests.

On this particular day, it was the very new, and relatively young, Roman Catholic bishop from Raleigh just down the road. Also in attendance, along with 400 or 500 students, were the members of the area's Baptist Pastor's Association, whose monthly meeting included attending chapel and dining in the cafeteria.

Well the bishop, who was from somewhere up north, was in the middle of a carefully researched and written homily on Christian unity when he said something like, "No matter what our differences, we are united in having been saved by the blood of Christ, and made alive by the gift of the Spirit," at which point several of the pastors got up, waving handkerchiefs and shouting, "Amen, Preach it! That's Right! C'mon!"

Manuscript pages shot up in the air and fluttered to the floor while a flustered and somewhat embarrassed bishop said gracefully, "I'm sorry. You have to understand. In the Catholic Church, no one says "amen" unless it's written in the worship book. I'll be ready next time."

PRACTICE

I have never been any good at things like playing a sport beyond the middle school level, or singing, or playing a musical instrument. Part of it is a lack of natural talent. But that's just part of it.

My biggest problem has been an unwillingness to practice, to go over and over the basic, rudimentary motions of any particular activity enough to get good at it. There were a couple of exceptions. I could shoot a fairly consistent 10-foot jump-shot in basketball and I became a pretty good contact hitter in baseball. But I was not a good player. I just wouldn't work at it.

 The same thing with music. I had no natural talent or ear, though I could have learned to be an adequate singer, but I wouldn't put in the dull, repetitious, monotonous time necessary. Same thing for the guitar I bought, and the piano lessons I signed up for.

It was only when my sons came along that I really learned what it took to be good at something. The oldest played trumpet and French horn in band. We had a small house. There was nowhere but his bedroom for him to practice and there was nowhere in the house one could go and not hear him. The same thing, over and over and over. But he stuck with it and became pretty good.

The youngest was in love with basketball. He developed his own practice routine, outlined on a chart on his bedroom wall; fifty lay-ups from this side, fifty from the other side, a hundred free throws, a hundred jump shots, etc. etc. There was a concrete patio directly outside the den door. We put up a goal there – it was maybe 20 feet from both the television and the kitchen sink. His dribbling and shooting and jumping reverberated through the house.

Sometimes they were both practicing at the same time; scales coming down the hall from the bedroom; thump, thump, thump from the backyard; for hours on end. And the last thing I was going to do was complain. I put in my earplugs and went back to working on my sermon.

One of the goals in sport is to make the regular activities such second nature that you quit thinking and just do it. To do that takes practice.

Which, I believe, is why we talk about "practicing our religion."

CALL STORY

In the part of the world where I grew up, the southern Appalachian Mountains, a minister is expected to have a "call story," the more "Damascus Road" dramatic the better. When I started seminary I did not have such a story and was therefore a bit of a disappointment to many of my more pious neighbors and relatives.

So, I made one up.

Instead of my usual lame, "Well, I've just always felt like it's what God wants me to do," I started saying, "I was in the tobacco field on a hot and humid day in late July. There had been a thunderstorm in the early afternoon so I had red mud up to my knees and there was steam coming off the tobacco leaves.

"I was hot, wet, and muddy when I looked across the creek to the paved road and saw a Ford Fairlane drive by with the windows rolled up and the air conditioning on. The man inside was wearing a white shirt and a thin black tie. He has patting the steering wheel and singing along to the gospel music playing on the radio.

"I looked up at the sky and said to God, 'Yes Lord. I can do that. I will do that. I will become a preacher.' "

I don't think anyone ever believed me but they did quit asking.

COMMUNION

Many years ago, when I was a young pastor, I was teaching a Catechism Class on a Sunday afternoon. A few minutes after we started, a young man came in, toting his four-year-old sister on his hip. "Mama has to go to the hospital to see Grandma. Says I got to keep Annie." "Which means I 'got to' keep Annie," I thought to myself as I heard his mother pull out of the church parking lot.

We were studying Holy Communion. I got Annie set up in the corner with a coloring book, then I began to go over the lesson with my three students.

Question – What two things make a Sacrament?
Answer – An Earthly Element and a Divine Command.

Q – What are the two Sacraments we observe? A – Baptism and Communion.

Q – What is the Earthly Element in Baptism? A -Water.

Q – What is the Earthly Element in Communion? A -Bread and Wine.

Q – What are the Bread and Wine? A – The Body and Blood of Jesus.

Q – So, when we eat the bread, what are we eating? A – The Body of Christ.

Q – And when we drink the wine, what are we drinking? A – The Blood of Jesus.

At this point I heard a noise in the corner, and turned to see Annie staring at us, wide-eyed. She loudly proclaimed "YEECH!"

Then she threw up.

DETAILS

My wife and I have been married for over forty years, and we met while we were still in high school. When you've been together that long, you have a lot of shared memories. Well, actually not so much. What you have is a lot of shared experience which you almost inevitably remember differently.

This situation provides a lot of, shall we say, "opportunity for vigorous conversation," which usually begins with, "I have no idea who you're talking about. You say we went to dinner with them in Nashville in the 1990s?" or "No, no, no; you've got that all wrong, it was in Hightower in 1979 – not China Grove in 1985." Trust me, sometimes this can go on half the night.

After forty plus years together, my wife and I do have trouble remembering the same details of our life together, or remembering the same details the same way – but we always remember we love each other and want the best for each other.

So, it is with God and us. We sometimes remember the story of God's love differently, we forget details others think are important, we harp on things nobody else cares about.

But underneath it all, we can be sure of one thing – The Maker of all things loves us all.

DRIVING ME-ME

Our now grown boys were elementary school age when we lived in the suburbs outside Atlanta.

My mother-in-law, known to the boys as "Me-Me," lived in eastern North Carolina. Every summer they spent several weeks with her on the farm. We often met for the "kid exchange" around Columbia, South Carolina.

I remember one year in particular that we had trouble finding each other. I had told Me-me to meet me at a particular gas station off a certain exit. I had been stalled by an accident and was running very late. When I got there, Me-me and the boys were nowhere to be found. This was well before the days of cell phones so we had no way to check in with each other. I decided she might have gone to the wrong exit and doubled back a bit.

Unfortunately, she had decided the same thing about me. Just as I got back on the interstate I spotted her car going up the ramp on the other side. After a serio-comic hour of trying to catch one another, we finally ended up in the same place at the same time.

After that, we decided that at all future meets, Me-me would stay put and I would look for her.

IT JUST IS

The most difficult course I took in college was "Art Appreciation." Not that it was all that difficult in itself, it was simply very difficult for me. Imagine a southern boy, fresh off the farm, sitting in a dark room with a tiny French woman showing slides and encouraging us to, "live into the painting."

"Let it speak to you," she chirped, "invite the art to commune with your spirit." To say I didn't get it would be a vast understatement.

I kept asking, with pen poised over paper to write down the definitive answer, "What does it mean?" and she continually replied, "It does not mean anything, it just is. Experience it with an open mind and see what you see." Suffice it to say, I didn't "commune" with many paintings that semester.

Over the following years, I found that many of the most important things in life have no definitive answer. The truth they have to offer comes to us only in the experience, not in the explanation.

SCIENCE GUY

My older son is a science guy; his parents, a preacher and a social worker, most decidedly are not. This became very clear to us one day when he was seven. My wife and the boys were fishing in a little pond in our sub-division. The sun was setting and the western sky was full of colors; red, purple, orange.

The four-year-old asks, "What makes the sky so pretty?"

Mom answers something about God creating natural beauty for our enjoyment and to remind us of the presence of the holy in the world around us.

And the seven-year-old says, "Well, Mom, actually it's just the sun reflecting off dust particles and moisture in the atmosphere."

Like I said – a science guy.

WRONG PLACE

One time when we were in college, my then-girlfriend (and now-wife) and I went from Chapel Hill, NC over to downtown Durham to the art-house movie theater to see some European movie with subtitles. We got lost several times and then had trouble finding parking and finally we rushed in for the show and got a seat.

By the time we settled in, the movie had already started. It was strange – the actors were really terrible and the dialog – such as it was – was in English, not Italian.

We looked at each other with puzzled faces and then, almost at exactly the same moment, it dawned on us that we were in the wrong place and how *really* wrong that place was.

We got up and got out quickly and went for pizza instead.

HELLO

I started my career as a pastor in three little churches in rural NC. Wood-frame buildings on isolated dirt roads, a few dozen farmers and shop-owners and their children and grand-children who drove out on Sundays from the cities to visit the folks and go to church.

One weekday noon I went into a church member's place of business for lunch: Alvis Brigg's Bar-B-Q.

As I walked in, a Briggs grandchild, a boy about 4 years old, spotted me. He stood up in the booth where he was sitting and yelled out, "Hello . . ." and then he was silent, because he couldn't remember where he knew me from.

He tried a couple more times, "HELLO . . ." then silence and meditation, "HELLO . . ." again, and more thoughtful silence. By this time everyone in the room was quiet and looking back and forth between the boy and me.

Finally, his face brightened and he shouted, "HELLO CHURCH!"

FIVE YEARS OLD

It was over twenty years ago. We were on one of those endless car trips from South Atlanta to Mount Airy NC for Thanksgiving weekend.

We finally got everything and everyone loaded up and ready to go and got on our way about three PM. With luck we'd be there before midnight.

About 30 minutes from home a little voice from the back seat piped up, "Are we there yet?"

"No, we're not there yet. We just left home."

Five minutes later, "Are we there yet?"
"No. Read your book."

Five minutes later, "Are we there yet?"
"No, I'll tell you when we get there."

After about fifteen or twenty more, "Are we there yet" inquiries, I exploded, "No! And if you ask me that question one more time you're in big trouble!" (One of my parental specialties was the ill-defined and unenforceable threat.)

After a blessed period of silence, a timid voice came from the back seat, "Will I still be five years old when we get there?"

Part 3: Living Life
(Out into the World)

"We do not remember days, we remember moments."

-- **Cesare Pavese**

"Life is 10 percent what you make it, and 90 percent how you take it."

-- **Irving Berlin**

AT THE OPERA

Almost every Saturday afternoon, I listen to the opera on the Public Radio Station.

Some of the people who know me might be surprised by this, though they shouldn't be. I like opera; not as much as I like Lynard Skynard or ZZ Top.

But I like opera.

Well, actually I don't like opera, but I do like the idea of liking opera; deep down inside I fell like an educated person SHOULD like opera, and sooo....

On Saturday afternoons I listen to opera, kind of on the same theory as your mother had when she kept feeding you liver and asparagus, hoping that one day you would come in and when she said, "What would you like for dinner?" -- you would say, "How about some yummy liver and asparagus?"

Not gonna happen, but hope springs eternal in the human breast.

Anyway, I listen to opera in the vague hope that someday I'll like it and can then count myself as a genuinely educated and cultured person. Every once in a while, I find myself liking a piece, nodding along and getting into it and thinking, "Gee, I beginning to like this opera stuff."

But then I realize that the opera pieces I liked were the ones they used as soundtracks for Bugs Bunny and Elmer Fudd cartoons, and I was back to square one.

It's not music appreciation; it's just nostalgia for my childhood. I'm still listening, and I'm still hoping, but I'm into my 60's now. I don't think this plan is working.

THERE YOU HAVE IT

Back in the early 80's, I spent a year doing post-M.Div. studies at the Lutheran Seminary in Columbia, SC.

One Sunday I was scheduled to preach in Pomaria, SC. (It was a long time ago, maybe it was Prosperity, or Pelion. It was one of the P's.)

I couldn't find the town or the church. Every road had a couple of brick Lutheran Churches, but none of them was the one I was looking for. It was less than 15 minutes before the service and I still couldn't find the church.

My moment of ultimate frustration came when the road I was on dead-ended into another road. There were two signs facing me, pointing in opposite directions, each saying, "Pomaria 5 miles."

There was a farmer in the corner of the field, working on his tractor. I rolled down the window and asked, "Does it matter which way I go to Pomaria?"

He looked at me, he looked at the signs, he spat on the ground and looked back at me, "Not to me it don't."

SAME TIME

A few weeks ago, I was browsing in a bookstore and I ran across two books I had never seen before.

One is *The Optimist's Guide to History;* the other is *The Pessimist's Guide to History.*

While I was checking out, the clerk looked over her glasses at me and said, "I've sold a lot of these books, but nobody's ever bought them both at the same time."

I said, "Well, I guess most people are either optimists or pessimists, but I'm just a preacher looking for sermon ideas."

And the Good News is: I found one.

The books are organized in chronological order, beginning with Creation, or the Big Bang, depending on your point of view; and progressing to the present.

The Optimist's Guide points out the positive events in history while the Pessimist's Guide lists all the horrors that have ever happened.

As I read through these two books, I noticed two interesting things.

> 1) The Pessimist's Guide is much longer than the Optimist's Guide; (360 versus 260 pages.) I don't know what that means, I just noticed it.

> 2) There are many things in each book which I, personally, would have put in the other book. Some things the authors counted as Bad, I saw as Good, and vice versa.

It would appear that whether something is Good News or Bad News is a tricky question.

It depends not only on whether or not you're an Optimist or a Pessimist, but also where you're standing when you look at it.

FINE PRINT

I am an acknowledged Luddite. Technology befuddles me. I still carry a fountain pen, my watch has a dial with numbers and a big hand and a little hand. I can't program a VCR or anything else. To me, a computer is a fancy typewriter and I treat it like one.

Often times even simple technology defeats me.

For instance, passenger-side rear-view mirrors. For the life of me, I can't figure out why they put mirrors there designed to deceive us.

It happened again last week. I was rushing up and down the interstates, over a thousand miles in three days. I looked in the outside mirror, plenty of room to move into the right lane. I slide over, horns blare, brakes screech, and I glance back over my right shoulder; there's a car even with my rear bumper in the right lane. Looking in the mirror, it seemed so very far behind me.

Then I read the fine print, the fateful words:

> ***Objects in mirror are closer than they appear.***

"Now, why do they do that?" I fumed.

BITS AND PIECES

My Daddy lived until he was 80. Until he went to the hospital a week or so before he died, he lived in the house he was born in.

The only time he spent any real time away from there was when he was in Europe in WWII.

He never told us much about it until the last year of his life, and then in bits and pieces.

Buddies who were there one minute and blown up the next, little French and German children stepping on mines or begging for food.

As I sat at that kitchen table, listening to him talk, coffee cup in one hand and cigarette in the other, I began to understand his years of staring into the distance, the emotional distance, the stoic devotion to duty.

Then he began to weep, his 80-year-old shoulders going up and down, as he cried for someone named Willie from Oklahoma.

And I cried for Willie and Daddy and millions of others, American and English and French, Korean and Vietnamese and Iraqi and Afghan, and all those caught up in the senselessness and pain.

MIGHTY WIND

In the fall of 2004, Hurricane Ivan hit the Gulf Coast with a fury that did not peter out until it reached the NC mountains. I know, I was there.

I had a group of young pastors meeting at a retreat center. It was their first week together. They were from all over the country.

It had been a good week, a getting to know you week, but on Thursday night, it became a very interesting week indeed. It had been raining all day and we knew a hurricane had hit the Gulf, but we were in the mountains, for God's sake.

We were safe.

After dinner, I went out and sat on the lodge porch and looked at the rain on the lake, trying to do some last minute program adjustment. Suddenly, I realized what was happening right in front of my eyes. I thought, "Look at that, little tornadoes, water sprites, dancing across the lake. And waves. Big waves. We don't have waves on mountain lakes."

Then it really hit. Trees bending toward the earth, electricity going out, roofs lifting up. Light pole breaking off 5 feet in the air, power lines dancing around on the ground.

And, in the midst of that, I had a stupid attack.

Someone came into the kitchen and said there was a tree down across the road that was the only way in and out of the Retreat Center. For some reason, he and I decided it was vital to get that tree off the road, in the middle of the hurricane.

So we got a chain saw and loaded a couple of young pastors in my old Jeep Cherokee, (Herb from South Dakota and I think John from Kentucky, I don't remember who else was along.) We drove down until we got to the place where the trees had fallen across the road and began to work.

The wind was blowing, the rain was falling, the trees were slick; we made some progress on one and moved up to the next one. And, then -- well it's kind of confusing but I've never been so scared in all my life, before or since.

The wind started blowing in a particularly hard and swirling manner, and the trees around us began to twist and twirl in the air, and to crack and moan and make noises both mournful and threatening. Just looking up into the twisting tree tops was a vertigo-inducing experience. Suddenly, I and all those with me knew ourselves to be in mortal danger and we ran to the seeming safety of the car.

Maybe it's a professional hazard, but the words of scripture comes to you at odd moments, sometimes:

> *And suddenly from heaven there came a sound like the rush of a violent wind and it filled the entire house where they were sitting. (Acts 2:2)*

So, here's my question. If the Holy Spirit is indeed like a "violent wind," like an untamed hurricane or a sudden and destructive tornado, what makes us think we want it in our lives?

FARMERS

Though I grew up on a farm and worked it quite a bit, truth is, I wasn't much of a farmer; just never really had any interest in it. I mean, I could do the work and I did it well. It just didn't excite me.

Frankly, I found the whole business, well, boring. It took too long, it was too unpredictable, too uncontrollable, too frustrating. Plow the ground, put in the fertilizer, plant the seed, chop out the weeds, and wait and wait and wait; and pray and pray and pray.

Pray for rain; pray it doesn't hail; pray for the rain to stop; pray for it to warm up; pray for it to cool off. While you're praying, you need to be spraying; spray for bugs, spray for weeds; praying and spraying for weeks on end.

And after all that, it's out of the farmer's hands anyway. No matter how hard you try, sometimes it doesn't work. Most of the time, it's too hot or too cold or too wet or too dry or prices are too high or too low.

If it's a good year, everybody has a good year and there's an oversupply of the crop and prices are too low. If it's a bad year; everybody has a bad year and supply is down and prices are high, but you don't have anything to sell.

In the end, there was too much luck involved for me to be a farmer. I wasn't a very good farmer because I didn't have the right disposition. I'm not patient enough. I'm not comfortable with the fact that success ultimately is in the hands of fate, or the weather, or God; depending on how you look at it.

GOLF THEOLOGY

Me, I'm lazy. I use golf theology. Used to play golf with a minister friend of mine and we came up with the term.

We got to thinking about all the people we knew who spent a lot of time on the golf course complaining about their lie, or trying to improve their lie, legally or, most often, illegally and sneakily, moving the ball out of sand traps and from behind tress when they thought no one was looking.

Or they were obsessing about their score, or they were trying to improve their score, or they were lying about their score, etc.

And we realized that neither of us worried too much about all that. We were just glad to be out of the office and out on the golf course, whacking away at the ball in the general direction of the hole.

Then, being preachers, we started thinking of all those pastor friends we knew who were always trying to improve their theological lie, trying to make things make better sense, etc.

And we decided that we were golf theologians; we preferred to take things as they came, to play it as it lay, to whack away in the general direction of heaven.

THE PASTOR'S DEAD!

I was driving back to the church after a hospital visit one wintry afternoon over 30 years ago. The sun was shining bright and directly into my eyes. I turned left at a lonely country intersection and BAM! My little Datsun was slammed into by a large delivery truck doing 60 miles an hour.

He hit me right behind the back door and the car spun round and round like a top, then WHAM! I stopped, wedged into the ditch on the side of the road.

Every window in the car was broken, the steering wheel was broken, the seat was broken.

My head was in the backseat, passenger side and my feet were under the steering wheel and I couldn't breathe. I literally COULD NOT BREATHE. That truck knocked the wind out of me.

The wreck was witnessed by one of my parishioners, Kitty Hightower. She ran to my car and leaned in the broken window. "Pastor, Pastor are you all right?"

Well no, I wasn't all right. I couldn't breathe. There was no air in my lungs and I didn't seem to be able to get any in there.

I couldn't speak, I couldn't even move; I just stared at her with my mouth open.

Kitty started crying, and then started screaming to the men rushing over from the country store, "He's dead, He's dead. Oh my God, the Pastor's dead!"

Which is, I assure you, a peculiar thing to have screamed in your ear when you are indeed very much alive.

After what seemed like an eternity I was able to get a bit of air into my lungs and was able to lift a hand and touch Kitty on the shoulder; which, in retrospect, was not the best thing to do, seeing as how she thought I was dead and all.

When I touched her on the shoulder, she jerked her head up and looked at me with real terror in her eyes.

Finally, I squeezed out the words, "It's alright Kitty, I'm not dead."

Bless her heart, for a minute there I wasn't so sure about Kitty!

BREAKFAST WITH JESUS

One day about 20 years ago, I went to a Holy Week breakfast at the big downtown church in a major southern city. It was a Chrism Mass and the Bishop had called us together to renew our ordination vows and to eat together.

We drove in early, most of us from the suburban and rural outskirts. We wore our best Lutheran finery, black suits and black shirts and white collars and silver crosses. We vested in the chapel and filed into choir stalls in the chancel where the bishop preached and prayed and gave us communion and we prayed and pledged our troth and received the elements with humble hands if not totally humble hearts.

We divested ourselves of our albs and stoles and then retired to the small dining room where the Altar Guild laid before us a brunch of eggs and bacon and biscuits and cheese grits and sausage balls and fresh fruit and, and, and. . . .

We sat at oak tables covered with linen table cloths and ate off good china with silverware that appeared to have a significant amount of real silver in it. And we had a wonderful time lamenting how difficult our lives were and how taxing our jobs were and what a burden Holy Week was and eventually it got time for me to leave.

Somewhere between the small dining room and the chapel where I recovered my alb and the long hallway to the parking lot, I got turned around and lost, and went downstairs and down a corridor and found myself spilling out into the street on the opposite side of the church from where I expected and wanted to be.

The morning sun was shining brightly in my eyes and it took me a moment to gather my wits and figure out where I was, and when I came to myself, I looked down the sidewalk in the direction I wanted to go and saw a long line of folk huddled on the dewy grass, trying to stay warm and dry while waiting for the food kitchen housed in the church's basement to open.

I felt very conspicuous walking along beside that row of folk, dressed in my best suit, carrying my white robe, a silver cross around my neck. I spoke to a few folk as I hurried past them to the corner. As I came to the street and turned to the left I glanced back and then I looked up and to my right. And what I saw stopped me dead in my tracks.

From where I stood, I could see in the floor to ceiling, wall-to-wall windows of the small dining room. I could see the assembled holy people of the area Lutheran churches, smiling and talking; warm, dry, and well-fed.

By simply shifting my eyes I could see a significant portion of the area's homeless population, cold, hungry, silent and appearing as alone in a group as they were by themselves.

And I wondered, "On this Tuesday in Holy Week, in this city, at this hour; which group would Jesus be eating with; the clergy or the homeless?"

Really, I wondered, "Which group should I be eating with?"

Or better yet, "Shouldn't all of us be down here eating with all of them?"

AUNT MILDRED

I have concluded that almost everyone has a relative like my late Aunt Mildred.

She was my Daddy's sister, she lived with her parents until they died, then she married her longtime suitor. She never had children, which, some of us think, was something of a blessing for those unborn.

Having no children, she doted on her nieces and nephews and sent us birthday cards with sticks of gum in them until we were well into our 30's and 40's. She also wrote long, disjointed letters all over those cards; front, back, and then folded them out and wrote on the inside.

One time, in the midst of all the news about Uncle LW's impending hernia surgery and what they had for lunch at the Derby and what they had to pay for it and what was wrong with it, and how Myrtle feels about her son's job change (now if I can only figure out who Myrtle is) and a long digression on the ugly dress Cousin somebody wore to Grandpa Watson's funeral in 1960, and a guess at how much rain they had last week based on the amount in the coffee can on the stump in the backyard, there was buried this line: **"I paid the premium on your Combine Accident Insurance last week."**

Believe it or not, that was the first thing in that letter that I did not understand at all. What? What is Combine Accident Insurance? A combine is a piece of farm equipment I haven't been near since I was twenty years old. And, I'm sure it's not about farm equipment anyway and what kind of insurance is it and why is Aunt Mildred paying the premium? In the midst of this muddle, I did what all southern boys who have been raised right do.

I called my mother.

She said, "Oh Lord, you know your Aunt Mildred, bless her heart. She takes out these policies on all you children all the time. She's scared to death somebody she knows will wind up in the hospital unable to pay their bills. She's got policies on all 5 of you children, plus LW's nieces and nephews, too. I tell her you all have got jobs and insurance but she just says it might not be enough, you can't ever have too much insurance."

I said, "Mama, what should I do? She's wasting her money!"

"Oh honey, there's nothing you can do. She's convinced that this Combine Accident Insurance is the greatest thing in the world and nobody can change her mind. If you ever have an accident, would you please let her know? Nothing would make her happier than to file a claim on you."

Though it did make me feel strange to learn that the best way to make Aunt Mildred happy was to get hurt, I decided that Mama was right and wrote Aunt Mildred a thank-you note and let it go.

THE NEWS

When my parents were still living, I used to call home about once a week. It was a "News from Lake Woebegone" sort of phone call – though in my case it was the "News from Slate Mountain."

I got an update on the latest spat at the church and how the weather and the crops were doing and finally the obituaries, which were always a bit confusing because I never really knew who was being talked about – neither who was dead nor who was mourning.

Daddy would say, "Well, I don't reckon you heard about William McCorkle* dying?"

While I was smart enough not to point out to my father that a 75-year-old man dying in Slate Mountain, North Carolina was unlikely to be big news in Atlanta; I was not smart enough to refrain from admitting that I did not know who William McCorkle was.

"Sure you do," he would protest, "He was your Great Aunt Vesta's first boy by her second husband, Old Man Willard McCorkle. She married him after your Great Uncle Grover Cleveland Chilton died."

Me: "I still have no clue, Daddy."

My father: "He ran that little store up on Highway 52, almost into Virginia."

Me: "Oh yeah, I remember him. He would sell beer to me when I was still underage and in high school."

Daddy: "Well, he wasn't a real Chilton, but anyway – he died. Funeral's at the Holiness Church on Tuesday."

* None of the names here are real, though the story is true enough.

I LIKE SMOKING!

A number of years ago, I served as the stewardship consultant for a friend's congregation, including being the "guest preacher" on Commitment Sunday.

The lectionary text for that Sunday was the story of the woman who had been suffering from hemorrhages for twelve years. In consultation with the pastor, I told him that I would find it difficult to preach on this text without offering the opportunity for people to come forward for anointing with oil and the laying on of hands for healing.

Though he was worried about the timing involved in adding the liturgy for healing to an already full agenda of two services with communion and the bringing forward of commitment cards, he agreed with my plan.

Things went well on Commitment Sunday. Not only did the congregation increase their pledges by a good percentage, we were pleased and a little bit surprised to see almost everyone in the congregation come forward for the laying on of hands.

A few weeks later I received a call from the pastor. He said, "Have I got a story to tell you."

He went to visit a man who has been visiting worship for the last few weeks. He lives in a boarding house just down the street. After a few minutes of pleasantries, he told the pastor that Commitment Sunday was the first time he visited the church. He had just gotten out of rehab and had committed himself to going to church.

He said, "I had never been to a Lutheran church before, but it was close and I had no car so I walked over. I went to the 8:00 service and decided to do whatever everybody else did, so when people went up for healing, I went too. And later I went up for communion. I even filled out one of those Commitment cards. I said I'd give as much as I could when I could. After service I went to coffee hour and an adult Bible class and then somebody invited me to come to the congregational dinner after second service, so I sat in the library and read until the dinner. Long story short – it was almost 3:00 pm when I got back to my room.

"When I walked in I saw my ashtray overflowing with butts and ashes and thought 'Gee, I haven't had a cigarette since before church.' so I lit one up. And it tasted terrible. I spit it out. And then I realized what had happened, why I didn't like cigarettes anymore. When you prayed for my healing, you asked me what I wanted to be healed of and I said 'My addictions.'

"Pastor, I didn't mean smoking. I like smoking!"

THEY KNEW IT WAS YOU

I live in a very small place, a county of less than 10,000 people with one town with fewer than 500. A few years ago, I was working at a United Methodist Retreat Center here and received the opportunity to write some short devotional pieces to be printed on the back of United Methodist church bulletins. It didn't pay much but I enjoyed doing it and my mama was a Methodist and it made her proud, so it was a good deal all around.

In the two years of the series I only saw a printed bulletin once and that's sort of a funny story. I occasionally heard from people around the country about the devotions. Friends were in Sunday worship were surprised to find my name on the back of their church bulletin. I got emails from New York and Massachusetts and Montana and Oregon and California; even one from Alaska.

One summer night my college age son had a friend over who was also home from college. I stuck my head in my son's room to say hello and the friend said, "Hey Rev. Chilton (he was a very polite young man,) I saw your devotion on the back of our Methodist church bulletin this morning. I thought you might like to see it. Good meditation."

As I looked at the bulletin in my hands he said something that made me laugh and made me wonder. "Yeah, Rev. Chilton, I sat down in church during the prelude and looked at the bulletin and saw your name and said to the people around me, 'Hey, that's Rev. Chilton from the Retreat Center. That's Joe's dad,' and all the people around me said, 'Oh no; that couldn't be him. We know him. It must be someone else. They'd never print something from somebody from around here.'

And excuse me Rev. Chilton but I said, "Exactly how many ministers named DELMER Chilton do you think there are in the world?' But they still said it couldn't be you, because they knew you."

HANGING OUT

I was ordained many years ago, in Fayetteville, North Carolina, in a church not far from Fort Bragg. An old college friend drove several hours to be there. After the service that evening, he gave me a ride to the house where I was staying with another friend during the clergy conference that was to begin the next day.

Our route took us through a part of town where "working girls" offered their services to GIs. We came to a stoplight, and they spotted me sitting there in his open-bodied Jeep. I was wearing a black suit and clergy shirt. Several of them came over to the car and began talking while we waited for the light to change to green. I said to my friend, "Get me out of here or this might be the shortest clerical career on record."

He laughed as we drove away and then he said, "Well Delmer, I'm just a lowly English teacher, and you know I don't go to church very much, but the way I read the Bible – aren't those the very people you're supposed to hanging out with?"

 I knew the man a long time and I always hated it when he was right.

TURN IT AROUND

A few years ago a young woman who had an appointment with me arrived a little early and was shown into my office to wait while I finished up a meeting down the hall. As I came into my office she turned from the wall where she had been examining my diplomas. She pointed at one of them and said, "What is 'Spiritual Direction'?"

I fumbled around for an answer and finally said something like, "People come in to see me and I listen to them talk about their life, sort of like going to a counselor but, instead of whatever therapist might say, a spiritual director tries to help people find where God is in their life."

"That's funny," she said, "I should think it would be more important for them to figure out where they are in God's life." (I was tempted to take the diploma off the wall and give it to her – with my name scratched out and hers written in.)

Things change when we turn the question around.

HEART OF GOD

About fifteen years ago I attended a funeral in Nashville. It was for the sister of a parishioner who was also an acquaintance of mine. It was a lovely and unique service, because this particular United Methodist Church was a lovely and unique congregation.

As I sat there listening to the prayers and the sermons and the family eulogies I thought to myself that Holy Saturday was a perfect day for a funeral. Just as the church sits uneasily poised between Jesus' death on Good Friday and the joyous news of the empty tomb on Easter Sunday morning – these family and friends sat in church that day, precariously balanced between the facts of her life and the hope of her resurrection.

The service was a little long by Lutheran standards and the room was a little warm, and some of the eulogizers took a little while to get to the point, and my folding chair was a little hard, and, well -- I started to get a little sleepy and distracted.

Anyway, I shifted my weight and stretched my neck and when I did I spotted something: up to the right, high up on the wall, almost to the ceiling, was a big, black, square speaker, tilted out from the wall. And there was something red squeezed in behind the speaker, wedged in between it and the wall. I stared at it for a while until I finally figured out what it was – a big, red, heart-shaped balloon. No doubt it had drifted up there during some congregational event and, either no one had ever noticed it, or else no one had been clever enough or brave enough or industrious enough to get it down.

Those familiar with Roman Catholic piety will easily figure out what popped into my mind: *The Sacred Heart of Jesus*. It was a strangely comforting thought for a protestant minister, the love of Jesus peeking down at us, half-hidden behind that speaker. As we gathered and shared very human thoughts and feelings about life and death and grief and hope, that red, heart-shaped balloon helped me remember that God was there too; mostly hidden, lurking in the background, looking in on us with love.

SUPER MARKET RACES

I remember a time back in the sixties, back in the days before cable TV and state lottery, back when we were all more easily entertained, they had the Super Market Races on TV. They were sponsored by a supermarket chain and worked something like this: they showed taped races from New York and California horse tracks and the stores ran specials and gave out prizes depending on which horse won.

My late father-in-law used to tell a joke about two farms boys (we'll call them Bill and Jack) watching the Supermarket race after supper one night.

Bill said, "I bet you $5 horse #3 wins."

And Jack said, "You're on!" Sure enough, #3 won.

Bill grinned and said, "Aw, I can't take your money. I saw it last night on the other channel and knew #3 won."

Jack replied, "Go ahead and take it. I saw it too, but I didn't think he could do it again."

ALIVE AGAIN

A few years ago, I ran into an old friend in a shopping mall in Raleigh, NC. It had been 20 years since we had seen each other while students at Duke Divinity and I wasn't sure it was him. He wasn't very sure about me either, especially since he had been laboring under the illusion that I was dead. We stared at each other for a long time and finally I spoke his name and identified myself and he turned as white as a sheet and sat down on a nearby bench.

As we sometimes say back in the mountains, he was "all shook up." Someone had told him I had died in a car accident. Well, actually, they told him about another Chilton from Surry County who had died and, not being familiar with the large number of Chiltons there are in those parts, he had somehow gotten the impression that it was me who passed.

Once we got that cleared up he said an interesting thing. "I had gotten used to the idea of your being dead. **It'll take me a while to get used to the idea of your being alive.**"

VERY WANTED

A few years ago one of my parishioners, a young woman who had recently moved to Nashville from somewhere in the Midwest, dropped by my office for a chat about her love life, or rather about the lack thereof. She brought along a personal ad she had seen in the *Nashville Scene*, a free weekly newspaper.

She wanted to know what I thought. She was planning to write one like it. Why she asked me, I don't know.

The last time I had a date with someone I was not married to, I was still too young to buy beer. I got married when I was 20 years old. Anyway, the ad read like this:

> *VERY WANTED: 30-ish drummer in rockabilly band like the Billygoats, with a romantic spirit, professional career, blue eyes, Episcopal.*

Is it just me, or does that seem a bit too specific?

SHRIVEN

When I was a kid growing up in Mount Airy, NC, I had absolutely no knowledge or experience of the church year. We had a Christmas play on the Sunday night before Christmas and Easter just kind of showed up one Sunday with no preliminaries and had more to do with Sunrise Service at the Moravian Cemetery and the Easter Egg Hunt during Sunday School and my sisters and mother having new dresses than anything else.

We were not a liturgical people.

My favorite place to shop when I was a kid was the Robby's Army/Navy Surplus store on Main Street. Most Fridays I went to town with Mama when she went to "get her hair fixed," and went to Robby's to look at manly men stuff and to occasionally buy a knife or a shirt or something.

Across the street from Robby's was Trinity Episcopal Church; a tiny stone building that seated maybe 50 people and had a Fellowship Hall downstairs. Every year I was fascinated to see the sign go up in their yard advertising "Shrove Tuesday Pancake Dinner and Ash Wednesday Service."

Two different days; one sign.

Nobody I knew could tell me what that was all about; not parents or teachers or even my preacher. The best anyone could do was my Baptist Deacon Grandaddy who said, "I reckon it's the way them Episcopalians has a revival and a fellowship dinner."

 Close enough, I'd say, for an opinion formed out of almost complete ignorance of the subject; a technique I have inherited and exploited with my children over the years.

At about the same time, I became acquainted with the New Orleans tradition of Mardi Gras, mostly through my devout Aunt Ethel, who gave me Evangelical Tracts and Paperback books for Birthday and Christmas presents until she died when I was forty. (She was still hoping I would turn my back on my obvious crypto-Catholicism and accept Jesus.)

It was in a somewhat lurid paperback description of the soul-saving work of the Rev. Bob Harrington, known to his admirers as the "Chaplain of Bourbon Street." The only religious effect it had on me was making me consider going into the Baptist Ministry just so I could attend New Orleans Baptist Seminary.

Eventually, I began to connect the dots between Shrove Tuesday and Mardi Gras.

The Oxford Encyclopedia of Christianity notes:

> On the eve of Ash Wednesday, the first day of Lent, the season of fasting, people first went to confession, to be "shriven," hence Shrove Tuesday, and then ate pancakes, to use up the ingredients forbidden during Lent. This turned into a longer period of pre-Lent celebration, known as Carnival or Mardi Gras.

Although I admit to having a little fun with this, I don't think it far-fetched of me to see the two different ways of observing this day as being more than a cultural difference between the repressed and dour English and Northern Europeans on the one hand and the more "party-hearty" attitude of the French and the other Mediterranean peoples on the other.

We all find it difficult to figure out how seriously to take sin; our own and that of others.

SANTA

A few years ago, I found myself (much against my will) in a huge shopping mall in Nashville a few weeks before Christmas. I was on the second floor, heading for the elevator. In front of me was a young family; man pushing a stroller and baby with one hand, carrying gift boxes with the other, woman balancing presents on her right arm and holding onto a four-year-old boy with the other. The boy was almost out of control; whining, kicking, crying, pulling, etc.

The family got into the glass elevator and before the door closed I saw the mother take the young man's chin and turn his gaze to the large open space on the first level. She said, "Look down there. Santa's watching you. Do you want him to see you like this?"

The boy stared at Santa and said, "I'll be good until I get past him."

FAMILY REUNIONS

I go to a lot of family reunions as a pastor, especially those that happen at the church after worship. People graciously invite me to stay for lunch and I seldom decline.

I remember one reunion when a woman had gotten all excited about doing the family history. So after dinner, she began to give everyone a report.

She started with the first settlement in North Carolina in the 1700's and worked her way back up the Great Wagon Road through the Shenandoah Valley of Virginia to the Pennsylvania Dutch area back over to Germany, to the time of Luther and beyond.

It was kind of interesting for a while, but it then dragged on and on for an hour and people started getting bored.

As usual, I was sitting with the teen-agers and as she drew to a close, she asked, "Did I leave anyone else?"

The kid next to me muttered, "Yeah, Adam and Eve."

THEM'S MY DOWNFALL

My late mother-in-law was always on a diet. And she was always cheating on it, eating things she knew she shouldn't.

When her daughter or her husband would find a wrapper from a drive-thru breakfast hidden in her purse, she would sigh and say -- in her soft, sweet, eastern North Carolina accent –

"Ah, biscuits; them's my downfall."

An empty package of cookies in the trash?

"Ah, Oreos; them's my downfall!"

A takeout plate from Wilber's Barbecue under the car seat?

"Ah, ribs; them's my downfall!"

So, what's your downfall?

COME TO THE WATER

One Sunday years ago, a woman came to see me in my office after service. She said, "Pastor, I have a grandson named Jimmy. You've never met him. He's 32. He ran away from home at 13. He's led a bad life. He's come to stay with me now. He's dying. He has a brain tumor and there's nothing they can do. He wanted to know if you would come and talk to him."

I went that afternoon. She took me into the living room, introduced me to Jimmy and left us alone.

He looked like an emaciated Hell's Angel: jeans, black tee-shirt, leather jacket, dirty ball cap perched on his chemo-bald head.

"A little boy trying to act tough," I thought.

He wanted to "get right with God" before he died, he said. He was pulling in every spiritual tradition he could think of. He wanted to make confession and get absolution like a Catholic; get saved and baptized by immersion like a Baptist, and get the Holy Spirit and speak in tongues like a Pentecostal.

I told him I would do the best I could. The confession/absolution and the baptism I was sure I could do; the Spirit thing was up to God.

I guess when you're staring death in the face, you don't want to leave any salvific stone unturned.

He started talking and talked for a couple of hours. His story was hard for me to hear; I never worked so hard at listening in my life. His sins were real, not imagined; his guilt was deserved, not imposed.

There was nothing exciting or interesting or titillating about his sins; they were the ordinary products of lust and desire and a real disregard for the welfare or rights of others. Here was the real character: a sinner!

And it was not humanly easy for me to pronounce forgiveness on his wasted life. He had no time for a true amendment of his life, no time to make restitution or do penance, no time for me to see if his change of heart was genuine. There was no point in corrective therapy, no time for behavior adjustment plans, no purpose to be served in berating him.

There was only time for the working of the Gospel: for repentance and forgiveness, for baptism and grace, for death and the promise of life.

So, I stifled my impulse toward either judgment or comfort and followed the ritual for Individual Confession and Forgiveness. I heard his confession, I decided it was genuine, I pronounced forgiveness. And we set a time and place for his baptism: the next day at 1:00 PM, in his uncle's above-ground swimming pool.

When I drove up the next day, the "community of faith" had already gathered.

Jimmy's relatives were standing on one side of the pool: stout, plain, sturdy, church-going people.

Jimmy's friends were on the other side: loud, brassy, somewhat sleazy bikers and carnies of questionable taste and character.

They had all come together to see Jimmy get baptized.

I went into the water first, Jimmy followed. I said, "I baptize you in the name of the Father and the Son and the Holy Spirit," and dunked him under the water.

He came up sputtering and cussing and said, "Damn -- that water's cold!"

And, on impulse, I said, "Oops, looks like that one didn't take," and dunked him again, much to the delight of all around.

The second time he came up, he grinned and held his tongue, hugged me, and then pulled me under.

It was a good baptism.

Part 4: Home Again

'Yes, what else but home?

It all depends on what you mean by home.

Of course, he's nothing to us, any more

Than was the hound that came a stranger to us

Out of the woods, worn out upon the trail.'

'Home is the place where, when you have to go there,

They have to take you in.'

'I should have called it

Something you somehow haven't to deserve.'

-- **Robert Frost**, *The Death of the Hired Man*

"Home is where the heart is."

-- **Pliny the Elder**

THE CHAIR

A few years ago, my brother Tony got our Aunt Mildred a motorized recliner that would push itself up into a standing position.

One day when he went to visit her she said: "Tony, I'm having a lot of trouble getting out of my chair lately."

Tony said, "Let me have a look at the motor."

She said, "That won't do no good. I never plug it in."

Tony responded, "Well, why-ever not?"

Mildred, nonplussed as usual, replied "Well, what if the electric power went out whilst I was a-laying back in it? I'd be stuck up there like a hog on a fencepost."

A GOOD MAP

My late father-in-law used to love to tell the story of a man, "a city feller from up in Raleigh," who got his rented fishing boat stuck on a sandbar along the Outer Banks of North Carolina.

When the Coast Guard rescued him, he kept saying he couldn't understand how it happened. He was experienced, he knew how to navigate; there must be something wrong with his map.

He was right. There was something wrong with his map. It was a place mat from "Captain Tony's Sanitary Fish Market" restaurant in Morehead City.

True enough, in order to find your way through life, you need a good map.

WIDE AROUND THE TREE

My grandfather had a very sly wit, one that snuck up on you. He used to tell a story about a man who died. They had the funeral at his home, with the preachers and immediate family on the porch, mourners standing in the yard and an open coffin in the back of a mule-drawn wagon.

After several sermons and much weeping and gnashing of teeth, the widow climbed onto the wagon seat next to the undertaker who drove the wagon up the hill to the family cemetery. The road went underneath the limbs of a very large oak tree and the wagon bumped heavily on an exposed root. At that moment, the "deceased" snorted and coughed and sat up in the casket – not dead but alive, having been in a deep coma, apparently.

Some years later, the man died again. His funeral played out exactly like the previous one.

As the wagon neared the oak tree, the widow leaned over and whispered to the driver, "Why don't you go wide around the tree this time?"

ENDINGS

When I was a kid, we always got to the movies late because, well, Daddy was Daddy and he was always late, and it was difficult to get five children anywhere together at the same time. We always came in after the movie was about a third over.

So we saw the end of the movie, then we waited in the theater while the ushers swept the floor and carried out the trash, and a new crowd came in, then we sat through the previews and the opening of the movie, then the whisper came down the row, "Let's go. This is where we came in."

And Papa Chilton and Mama Chilton and all the embarrassed little Chiltons would file out.

Besides the embarrassment, the thing that stuck with me about that recurring experience was how odd it was to watch the beginning of the movie when you had already seen the end.

Knowing how the story comes out changes how you see the beginning.

TOBACCO

On a visit to my mother on the farm where I grew up in the foothills of Virginia, I went for a drive to check on old familiar places. Leaving the parking lot of Hatcher's Chapel United Methodist, I glanced down the road and across a pasture at the Pentecostal Church and remembered a story my late father had told me about that church. It brought a smile to my face as I stood at his grave later that day.

Most of the denominations in that part of the world were against tobacco, but the vast majority ignored the fact that many of their members were tobacco farmers or worked in tobacco factories.

Not the Pentecostal Holiness. They took their anti-tobacco stance seriously.

Daddy told me that every spring, when the farmers in his congregation planted their tobacco, the Preacher would go and see them and read them the section in the Pentecostal Holiness Discipline forbidding involvement in "the tobacco trade" and a scripture passage from Matthew about having two or three witnesses.

A few weeks later he brought two elders with him and did it again. And some time before Memorial Day, the women and children of the congregation gathered in solemn assembly to excommunicate their fathers and husbands and brothers, etc. Then everyone would go home to a nice Sunday dinner.

Sometime in the Fall, after everyone had harvested their crop and sold their tobacco, the women and children would gather again and vote their menfolk back in, just in time, my father added with a wink, for the church to collect a tithe on the proceeds of the tobacco sale.

HOME

My mother told me a story she had heard about a family in her community during the housing shortage of World War II.

A woman recalled that when she was about ten, she and her family were forced to live in two rooms as a friend's house because there was nothing else available.

One morning at church a very nice lady said to her five-year-old sister, "You're such a lovely family. It's too bad you don't have a home."

The little girl thought a minute then blurted out, "Oh we have a home. We just don't have a house to put it in."

MIZ GEORGE

My fourth grade teacher was a woman known as "Miz George." This was not Miss, for she was married, not Ms., for though she was quite liberated, she wasn't a modern feminist. It was not Mrs. – just good old-fashioned, general purpose, Southern Miz George.

The last time I saw her was at my Daddy's funeral several years ago. She came with my second grade teacher, Miz Collins. They taught the four oldest Chilton children at Redbank Elementary School in Claudville, VA, which is the reason none of us will ever end a sentence in a preposition or say "can," when we mean "may."

When I saw Miz Collins and Miz George at the funeral, I was reminded of how well they took care of us, their little flock of illiterate sheep, oh, so many years ago.

They did more than teach us the rudiments of grammar and the building blocks of mathematics. They also taught us to tuck in our shirts and to say "Yes, Ma'am" and "No, Sir," and "Please" and "Thank you."

They taught us to respect ourselves and to respect others. They kept us safe, they lead us beside the still waters of knowledge; they created a space in which our minds could grow.

They were good shepherds.

SEEING IN THE DARK

I took a number of trips over the years to see my Daddy and my Mama in the old farm house out in the country from Mount Airy, NC. As I'd head out the two-lane road from town to the farm, I'd start to notice that every farm had what I grew up calling a "pole light" — an electric light that illuminated the farmyard all night. I played a game with myself, trying to see if I could find a place in that 8-mile stretch where I was out of sight of one of those lights. It couldn't be done. All the way out into the country, a new yard light would appear up ahead before the last one was out of sight in my rear-view mirror.

So, I changed games. I decided to count the houses that didn't have a pole light. Again, it couldn't be done. Every house, every shed, every trailer and barn was awash in the purplish florescent glow of pole lights. Every one, that is, except Daddy's. There was that big old farm house, sitting forlorn and silent and DARK in the middle of a field, not a speck of light visible except a night light near the kitchen window.

As I pulled into the driveway, I laughed quietly to myself, "Leave it to Daddy to be the only person for miles around too cheap to have a light in the yard." I got out of the car and gathered my things, and being too cheap and too careless to own a flashlight, I stumbled through the dark toward the back door. I fell over the lawn-mower and raked my shins over the well-house, and bloodied my nose by walking directly into the corner of the house.

Finally, I stumbled into the house and Daddy called out from the bedroom, "Well, you're here then, are you? Cut that light out in there. It's burning 'lectricity."

Sometime the next day I pointed out to Daddy that his was the only house on the road without a yard light and, as politely as I could, I asked him why he did not have one. He looked at me, rubbed his nose, took a deep drag on his cigarette and said, "Well son, I was born in this house almost 80 years ago, in this very room. I've lived here my whole life. I know where everything out there is, so I don't see as how I need a light."

In that moment, as I realized that pointing out to Daddy that other people might need a light to get around in his backyard was unlikely to be a persuasive argument, I let it go and forgot about it.

UNCLE HARRY'S CLOCKS

A few years ago, I went home to the farm to attend a family reunion: the Hubbards, my Mama's people. While I was there I took a little side trip to go out to the church cemetery where my Mama and Daddy and his parents and grandparents and, well – you get the idea – that's where they're all buried. On the way to the cemetery I drove by my great-uncle Harry's place and my wife said, "Isn't that where the uncle lived who had all the clocks?" And so it was.

My uncle loved mechanical clocks and pump organs. He spent a considerable amount of energy looking for clocks and organs. He expended an equally considerable amount of money acquiring said clocks and organs. And he spent most of the last 20 or 30 years of his life repairing and maintaining those clocks and organs. Last estimate I heard was that he had over a hundred clocks and 13 organs in that old house when he died.

One day a man had come to deliver heating oil or diesel fuel for the farm machinery and he had come into the kitchen to get my uncle to sign for the shipment. Just as he prepared to leave, all 100 clocks went off. He was so amazed that he asked if he could stay until the next hour so that he could hear them all go off again. Nothing could have pleased my uncle more. He took the man on a tour of the house, showing his grandfather clocks and mantle clocks and table clocks and railroad cloaks, etc., etc. And when he ran out of clocks, he sat down and played a few hymns on one of the pump organs he had restored.

The time came for the clocks to chime and the driver of the delivery truck sat as if in a trance, listening with his heart as well as his ears. He got up from the table and said to Uncle Harry, I have several more stops to make. Would it be all right if I brought my wife and children back tonight so they can hear this?" And of course Harry said yes. When the man returned that night, he sat through another couple of sessions of chimes ringing. And after that, he always timed his visits to make sure he got to hear the chimes go off.

WHAT HAPPENED?

When you see the Southern Appalachian Mountains in the fall, you remember that it's just a great time and place to go out and participate in nature, even if your level of participation is simply to gaze at the mountains and rivers, the lakes and leaves, from the comfort of your car.

As you drive the narrow, winding roads around "Hanging Dog" and "Squirrel Ridge" and "Vengeance Creek" communities, you occasionally come upon an old farm house, perhaps with an out building or two.

The porch may be fallen in, the glass in the windows broken or missing, the tin roof of the barn mostly blown off, with a long, rusty piece of tin flapping up and down in the wind above rotting timbers. Weeds grow tall in the yard, saplings have pushed their way through the decaying floor of the house and branches poke out of doors and windows.

It is a sad sight for someone like me who grew up in such a house. One is left to wonder: what happened? Did the parents die and the children move away, having no interest? Did they go bankrupt and the farm was taken over by people with no interest in the farm but only in the land?

Sometimes, you just don't know.

FLOWER SERVICE

My father died about ten years ago. At his funeral, my cousin and her husband sang a song he had asked them to sing, an old mountain tune called, "Don't Bring Me Flowers When I'm Dead." I smiled to myself as they sang, thinking the song a perfect choice by my daddy to sum up his theology, his straight-forward way of dealing with others, and his musical taste.

Some of my good Lutheran friends, who had never experienced an Appalachian Methodist/Baptist funeral and were unfamiliar with the folk "hymnody" of the region, were puzzled by the whole thing.

I explained to them that the song had in mind a tradition still carried on in some small mountain churches of what is referred to as the "Flower Service."

(This is not to be confused with "Decoration Day" when people bring flowers to decorate the graves in the church cemetery.)

At the flower service, everyone brings a bouquet of flowers and places them on a table in front of the pulpit. These are not arranged bouquets; they are a large fistful of flowers from the garden and wild flowers from the fields and woods. Then the minister preaches a sermon on Matthew 5:23-24, stressing the need for harmony and peace in the congregation and reminding people of Our Lord's admonition to make peace with our neighbor before kneeling at the altar to pray to God.

After the sermon, a genuinely amazing "passing of the peace," takes place as everyone in the congregation comes to the table and retrieves their bouquet and then begins to go to every other person in the church to apologize for any hurt feelings or harsh words or misunderstandings.

From the oldest to the youngest, everyone talks to everyone else, not caring how long it takes. After apologies and words of forgiveness and reconciliation have been spoken and heard, people then exchange flowers, sealing the restoration of their relationship and then moving on to another sister or brother in Christ.

Which brings me back to Daddy's choice of this song for this funeral.

My father was not a perfect man; but he was the most honest man I have ever met. It was his firm conviction that if we would tell each other the truth and deal honestly with one another at all times, we would have very little need for either remorse or regrets.

If you need to make peace with me, the song says, bring the "flowers" now – as in the flower service. Don't hold on to your grudge and then salve your conscience with a nice spray at my funeral.

I HOPE IT'S TRUE

I have, in my thirty-six years as a pastor, lost count of the number of funerals I have conducted, probably in the range of three or four hundred.

And at every one I have assured the family of the promise of the resurrection. I have preached it, I have counseled it, I have prayed it, I have believed it.

When my Daddy died, I walked up to the coffin and saw him there, waxy and still, cold and formally attired in white shirt, tie and dark suit.

I stood there a moment and all I could think was "I sure hope it's true, this resurrection business I've been preaching all these years. I sure hope it's true."

GOOD AS WE DO

A woman I know had a brother who was one of the most worthless and trifling human beings I ever met. He was mean to his wife, ignored his children, avoided honest work like the plague, and was known far and wide as the biggest and most brazen liar in half a state.

One day, "Grandma" – as she was known – and one of her grand-daughters were sitting on the front porch; they were rocking, shelling peas and gossiping about the brother. The young woman maintained that her uncle was beyond hope and a serious embarrassment to herself and every other member of the family. She filled Grandma in on his latest episodes of public sorriness.

Grandma just rocked and shelled and nodded and listened and finally she said, "I'm sure everything you say is true. Still, Jesus loves your Uncle."

The granddaughter turned red in the face and sputtered, "I doubt that, I don't think even Jesus could love him."

"Yes child," Grandma said, "Jesus loves everybody and Jesus loves your uncle too.

Then she stopped rocking and shelling and sat perfectly still, while she stared off across the hills. "' Course," she said, almost to herself," that could be 'cause Jesus don't know him as good as we do."

THE TELEPHONE

I am reminded here of my Aunt Mildred on the telephone.

After a long gossip session, she would say, "Well, I would tell you more, but I already told you more than I heard myself."

At least, that's what Uncle LW said she said....

About the Author

Delmer Chilton hails from Patrick County in Virginia, just across the state line from Surry County, North Carolina. The house on the family farm that he grew up on straddled the line, making him one of the few persons in the world who can claim to have grown up in two places at the same time.

At any rate, he counts himself a Tarheel, having attended the University of North Carolina, Chapel Hill. Further educational pursuits took him to Duke University Divinity School and the Graduate Theological Foundation for advance degrees.

He has served as an ordained minister in both the United Methodist Church and the Evangelical Lutheran Church in America. He is the husband of Deborah, and the father of Lowell and Joseph.

Delmer's work can be read online weekly at LivingLutheran.com and LectionaryLab.com.

About the Co-author

John Fairless is the second half of the writing/teaching team that has come to be known as "Two Bubbas and a Bible." A lifelong Baptist and unrepentant Tennessee Volunteer, John is the husband of Sheila, parent of William, Christopher, and Kayla – and is Grandaddy to his beloved, Katie Mae.

Cover Photo: "Surry Gothic," from the Chilton Family Archives

Pictured: Seated, center, Emma Watson Chilton; standing, l to r, Mildred Chilton Anderson, Lowell Chilton, and Reid Chilton